CONTENTS

CONTENTS

CONTENTS

CONTENTS

CONTENTS

Take it with a grain of salt

Meaning:

Not everything you hear is always completely true. It's good to have some doubts and think carefully before believing everything you're told.

Origin:

The origin of this expression dates back to Ancient Rome. It was used by the Roman writer Pliny the Elder in the year 77 AD.

Example:

When Timmy said he saw a flying car, his sister listened but took it with a grain of salt.

In the same boat

Meaning:

We're all in this together, facing similar challenges. Like a boat, we must work as a team to overcome our difficulties.

Origin:

Many years ago in old Europe, people used big boats on rivers to travel. These boats were heavy wood with no motor. They needed everyone helping push with sticks.

Example:

When both Billy and Susie couldn't go to the party because they were sick, their mom said "Don't feel bad, you're both in the same boat!"

Break the ice

Meaning:

It means to start a conversation or friendship by doing something friendly or fun to make people feel comfortable and open to talking.

Origin:

The phrase is believed to have originated in 16th century England, but the exact details of its first usage are uncertain. It is commonly used to describe starting a conversation or communication between people.

Example:

They talked about their favorite toys to break the ice and become friends.

Go the whole nine yards

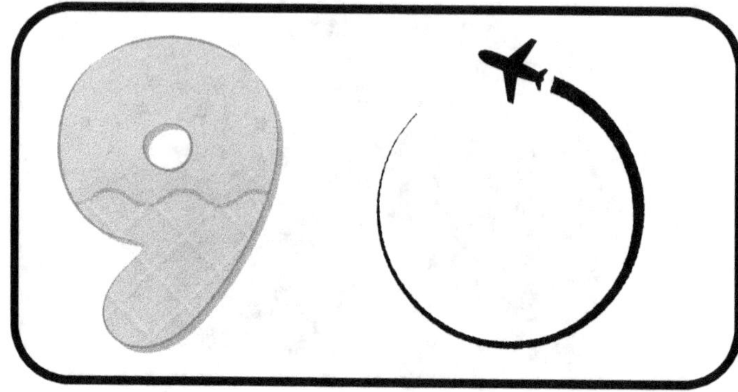

Meaning:

It means to give your best effort and do everything you can to accomplish something.

Origin:

Some suggest it relates to the length of ammunition belts on World War II aircraft, while others propose a connection to construction or fabric. However, these are speculative and lack concrete evidence. The true origin remains unknown.

Example:

He cooked a delicious meal, set the table beautifully, and went the whole nine yards to impress his guests.

In a nutshell

Meaning:

It means to explain something in a very brief and simple way, giving only the most important details.

Origin:

It is widely believed to have originated in England. Francis Bacon's work "Essays" includes a section titled "Nutshells," which indicates early usage of similar phrases in England.

Example:

The teacher explained the whole history lesson in a nutshell so they would have time for activities too.

Get off your high horse

Meaning:

It means to stop acting like you're better than others. Treat everyone fairly and with kindness.

Origin:

It is generally believed to have emerged in England during the 18th century.

Example:

She finally got off her high horse and apologized for her rude behavior.

Time flies

Meaning:

Time goes by quickly. Sometimes, when we're doing something fun or enjoying ourselves, we might feel like time is flying. It reminds us to make the most of important moments in our lives and use our time wisely.

Origin:

"Time flies" comes from the Latin proverb "Tempus fugit," meaning "time flees" in English. It's found in the works of Roman poet Virgil, particularly in his poem "Georgics."

Example:

Summer vacation went by so quickly! Time flies when you're having fun.

When pigs fly

Meaning:

The idiom means that something is so unlikely to happen that it's almost impossible. It's like saying that it will never happen because it's just too unbelievable or unrealistic.

Origin:

The origin of "When pigs fly" probably dates back to the Middle Ages. During that time, the idea of flying pigs was considered impossible or highly improbable.

Example:

They said they'll clean the entire house in five minutes when pigs fly.

On the same page

Meaning:

When we all understand and agree, it's like we're all thinking and working together towards the same goal.

Origin:

In the past, people read paper books without computers. If friends read different pages, they discovered different stories. But when pages matched, friends read in harmony.

Example:

The friends decided to play a game together, and they all agreed on the same rules. They were on the same page.

Fish out of water

Meaning:

Being in a situation where someone or something is out of their natural environment or feels uncomfortable or out of place.

Origin:

This usage began in England in the 1700s to describe the difficulties of fish without their lifgiving liquid habitat.

Example:

Sarah, a native English speaker, felt like a fish out of water when she traveled to a non-English speaking country.

Butterflies in my stomach

Meaning:

This expression is used to describe the feeling we get in our stomach when we are excited, nervous, or anxious.

Origin:

It is an idiomatic expression that originated in 19th century America, inspired by ancient beliefs about the human body.

Example:

The roller coaster ride gave me butterflies in my stomach.

It takes two to tango

Meaning:

To accomplish something effectively, both parties involved must contribute and work together. It implies that a joint effort and cooperation are necessary for achieving a desired outcome.

Origin:

This expression originated in Argentina, the birthplace of the tango dance. Tango emerged in Argentina around the late 19th century and gained popularity worldwide.

Example:

Doing something with a friend makes it more enjoyable because it takes two to tango!

All roads lead to Rome

Meaning:

This idiom means there are many ways to reach a goal or destination, emphasizing that different paths can lead to the same outcome.

Origin:

The idiom comes from the powerful Roman Empire. As the capital, Rome had many roads leading to it from different countries.

Example:

Just as there are many pieces in a puzzle, all roads lead to Rome, teaching us that there are different ways to solve problems.

Better late than never

Meaning:

Late is better than never. It's important to take action, even if it's delayed, rather than not doing it at all.

Origin:

The usage of the idiom may be traced back to William Shakespeare's play "The Merry Wives of Windsor" (1597), where the line "Better three hours too soon than a minute too late" appears.

Example:

I forgot to wish my friend a happy birthday, but I sent a belated card instead. Better late than never!

A piece of cake

Meaning:

Imagine a task that's super easy, like a walk in the park. That's what "A piece of cake" means. It's something so simple that even kids can understand.

Origin:

According to one theory, the idiom originated from the bakery culture in the United States during the 19th century. At that time, eye-catching and easily consumable cakes were displayed in bakery showcases.

Example:

The math problem was a piece of cake for him; he solved it in seconds.

It's raining cats and dogs

Meaning:

When it's raining really hard, it feels like the rain is coming down in a big, big way.

Origin:

During the Middle Ages, roofs were thatched with straw, and stray animals like cats and dogs would climb up for shelter. When it rained heavily, they could fall off, giving the impression of animals falling from the sky.

Example:

We had to cancel our picnic plans because it started raining cats and dogs.

Barking up the wrong tree

Meaning:

Searching in the wrong place or focusing on the wrong thing is like barking up the wrong tree.

Origin:

In the past, hunters used dogs to locate prey. Sometimes, the dogs would bark up the wrong tree, indicating the prey was elsewhere.

Example:

They thought the cat knocked over the plants, but they were barking up the wrong tree.

Every dog has its day

Meaning:

Everyone gets their chance to be happy and successful.

Origin:

The origin of this expression dates back to ancient Rome. Romans believed that even street dogs could occasionally achieve luck or success. In Rome, there were dog competitions held as part of certain events.

Example:

The math problem was a piece of cake for him; he solved it in seconds.

All that glitters is not gold

Meaning:

Don't judge things by how they look; they might not be as good as they seem.

Origin:

The origin of the phrase "All that glitters is not gold" can be traced back to William Shakespeare's play "The Merchant of Venice." The play, written around 1596-1598, features a character named Portia who delivers this line.

Example:

The shiny rock I found in the garden wasn't actually a valuable gem. Remember, all that sparkles is not precious.

Clean as a whistle

Meaning:

It means something is very clean and has no dirt or mess. It's like a whistle that makes a clear, sharp sound.

Origin:

One theory suggests that the phrase is associated with wind instruments from the 18th century. Instruments like the flute or whistle produce clean and clear sounds as air passes through them.

Example:

The car wash did a fantastic job; now my car is as clean as a whistle.

Elephant in the room

Meaning:

It's when there's a big, obvious thing everyone sees, but no one talks about.

Origin:

The exact origin of this expression is not known, but according to some theories, it dates back to the 20th century in the United States. This phrase refers to a situation where there is a big and obvious presence, like a real elephant in a room, but people choose to ignore it.

Example:

The broken vase on the shelf was the elephant in the room that nobody wanted to acknowledge.

Let sleeping dogs lie

Meaning:

Sometimes it's best to leave things as they are and not make them worse.

Origin:

One theory suggests it originated in England, although the specific year of its first use is unknown. The expression conveys the idea of not disturbing or bothering a situation where dogs are sleeping.

Example:

Your brother is already upset about losing the game. It's better not to mention it again. Let sleeping dogs lie.

All ears

Meaning:

It means that someone is very interested and attentive to what someone else is saying. It's like they have big ears that are listening to every word

Origin:

One theory suggests that "All ears" comes from a 16th-century English theatrical term, "pricked up his ears," which aimed to grab the audience's attention or listen carefully.

Example:

Whenever Grandma tells her life stories, I become all ears, fascinated by her adventures.

Get your ducks in a row

Meaning:

Being organized means getting everything ready and in the right order before starting something.

Origin:

This expression is believed to have originated in the late 19th century in the United States. It remains widely used today and is particularly helpful when there's a need to accomplish numerous tasks within a limited timeframe.

Example:

Sarah organized her crayons and pencils to get her ducks in a row for coloring.

Monkey see, monkey do

Meaning:

When we see someone do something, we might want to do it too. It's like copying what others do. It shows that people tend to imitate what they see.

Origin:

During the Warring States period (475-221 BC) in ancient China, a village monkey imitated the actions of the villagers. People found it amusing. This story explains the origin of the phrase "Monkey see, monkey do."

Example:

During a traffic jam, all the drivers on the road are in the same boat, experiencing delays.

Cry wolf

Meaning:

It's like when someone keeps lying about danger to get attention, but when a real danger comes, nobody believes them because of their past lies.

Origin:

The expression "Cry wolf" derives its origin from Aesop's fable "The Boy Who Cried Wolf." This fable is a very old tale that dates back to Ancient Greece.

Example:

The boy cried wolf so many times that when he actually needed help, nobody believed him.

Go the extra mile

Meaning:

It means to make an additional effort or do more than what is required. It's like going beyond what is expected to achieve a better result or help someone in a special way.

Origin:

The origin of this expression stems from a saying attributed to Jesus in the Bible, "If someone asks you to go one mile, go with him two miles."

Example:

Jack volunteered to stay late at work and go the extra mile to finish the project ahead of schedule.

Throw in the towel

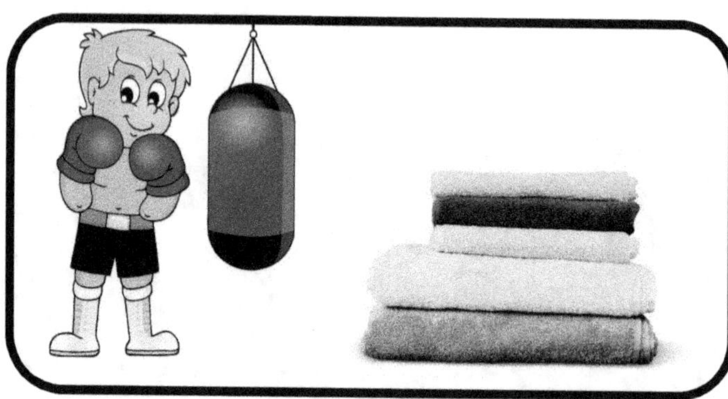

Meaning:

It means to give up, quit, or stop trying when faced with a difficult situation or challenge. It's like saying, "I can't do it anymore" or "I give up."

Origin:

This expression is believed to originate from boxing, where a coach throws in a towel to signal the boxer's defeat and surrender.

Example:

The little boy tried to climb the tree, but after a few unsuccessful attempts, he threw in the towel and came back down.

In hot water

Meaning:

Being in a tough spot or facing a problem with potential consequences.

Origin:

The phrase "in hot water" is believed to come from 17th century England and the popular hot baths of that time. Unauthorized entry into these baths often resulted in trouble. This association led to the expression "in hot water," meaning being in a difficult situation.

Example:

Billy accidentally broke his sister's favorite toy and found himself in hot water.

Don't cry over spilled milk

Meaning:

When things don't go as planned, it's better to stay positive and find a solution instead of getting upset.

Origin:

In the past, milk was important for nutrition, especially during the Middle Ages. Getting milk was hard work on farms, and spilling it meant losing something valuable. Instead of crying, people believed it was better to clean up the spill and move on to other things.

Example:

Emily made a mistake in her drawing, but she didn't cry over spilled milk and started a new one.

The ball is in your court

Meaning:

It means that the responsibility or decision-making power has shifted to you. It's like when playing a game and the ball is passed to you, it's your opportunity to take action.

Origin:

It might have come from a game like tennis, where the ball is sent to the other side and it's their turn to respond. It means it's their job to take action now.

Example:

You can decide what toppings to put on your pizza. The ball is in your court.

Castles in the air

Meaning:

It means to have big dreams or plans that are not based in reality. It's like building something in the air, it looks great from far away, but it's not really there.

Origin:

The origin of the phrase "Castles in the air" is based on the expression "building castles in the air" found in the 1817 novel "Guy Mannering" by the English writer Walter Scott.

Example:

Sarah's plan to eat ice cream for every meal is nothing but castles in the air.

Jump on the bandwagon

Meaning:

Follow the crowd: To join others in doing or liking something just because it's popular or trendy.

Origin:

In the 19th century, politicians in the United States traveled from town to town on wagons with marching bands during elections. It was a way to become popular and gain supporters, which led to the origin of this expression.

Example:

All my friends started collecting stickers, so I jumped on the bandwagon and started collecting them too.

The apple of my eye

Meaning:

This expression means that someone is loved and valued very much.

Origin:

Long ago in medieval times, when "apple" meant something dear, this fruit showed wisdom, affection and beauty. So people may have used this image to name the person cherished most of all in their heart, above all others.

Example:

The puppy we adopted has become the apple of our eyes. We can't imagine life without him.

Crocodile tears

Meaning:

Crocodile tears, when someone pretends to cry or show sadness but doesn't genuinely feel it. It's like fake crying to fool others or pretend to be emotional.

Origin:

The story goes that a long time ago, people believed that crocodiles shed tears to trick their prey. These tears were not real tears of sadness, but a cunning trick used to catch their victims.

Example:

The cat pretended to be sad with crocodile tears when it got caught stealing food from the kitchen counter.

A sight for sore eyes

Meaning:

It is an idiom that means "something that is very pleasant to see after a long time." It can be used to describe a person, place, or thing.

Origin:

It means seeing something that brings joy or relief. It originated in England and comes from an old saying about pleasing or comforting sights.

Example:

The ice cream truck on a hot day was a sight for sore eyes.

A drop in the bucket

Meaning:

It means a very small part of something big or a small action that doesn't have a significant impact.

Origin:

The first recorded use of this idiom was in the 17th century, in a book called "The Anatomy of Melancholy" by Robert Burton. He wrote, "A drop in the bucket, a small matter, a trifle." So, it's been around for a pretty long time!

Example:

A single raindrop is just a drop in the bucket compared to the heavy rainstorm outside.

Easy as pie

Meaning:

It means something is very simple or easy to do, like a piece of cake.

Origin:

The phrase "Easy as pie" has been widely used in the United States since the mid-19th century.

Example:

Solving a puzzle with only a few pieces is easy as pie compared to a big puzzle.

Butter someone up

Meaning:

To be extra nice to someone in hopes they'll help you or give you what you want.

Origin:

In ancient India, during certain religious festivals, offerings to the gods often included butter. The butter was used to appease the gods or establish a closer connection with them.

Example:

Mark helped his mom clean the house to butter her up and get permission to go to the park.

Birds of a feather

Meaning:

People who are similar or have similar interests tend to stick together and be friends.

Origin:

"Birds of a feather" idiom, origin in England and became popular in the 16th century.

Example:

Sarah and Emma are birds of a feather; they always wear matching outfits.

Cool as a cucumber

Meaning:

Being very calm and relaxed, just like when you take a deep breath and feel peaceful inside.

Origin:

The exact origin of the idiom "Cool as a cucumber" is not known, but it is believed to have originated in England during the 17th century.

Example:

Jack was nervous before his piano recital, but once he started playing, he became cool as a cucumber.

Bite your tongue

Meaning:

When you want to say something that might hurt or upset someone, it's better to stay quiet and not say it.

Origin:

The idiom "bite your tongue" originated in ancient Greece. The phrase was used in Greek drama, specifically in the play "The Clouds" by Aristophanes, written in 423 BCE. In the play, the character Strepsiades says, "I will bite my tongue and keep silent, lest I say something foolish."

Example:

He bit his tongue and didn't complain when his mom made him do extra chores.

Miss the boat

Meaning:

To miss the boat means to be too late or to miss an opportunity. It's like arriving at the train station after the train has already left.

Origin:

"Miss the boat" phrase is believed to have originated in the late 19th and early 20th centuries in the United States, specifically during the popular gold mining era on the West Coast.

Example:

Tina missed the boat to buy the last piece of cake, and it got sold out.

A crack in the wall

Meaning:

Even a small problem can lead to bigger troubles.

Origin:

The origins of this idiom can be traced back to the 15th century. During this time, construction materials and techniques commonly led to cracks forming in walls. Small cracks had the potential to worsen over time and compromise the integrity of walls or cause collapse.

Example:

Similar to how a crack in the wall weakens it, small lies can weaken trust between friends.

Keep your shirt on

Meaning:

Stay calm and be patient, just like taking a deep breath when things get tough.

Origin:

Although the exact origin of the expression is unknown, it is commonly believed to have originated in English slang during the 19th century.

Example:

Peter, don't get upset about losing the game. Just keep your shirt on and try again next time.

Let's call it a day

Meaning:

It means we're done for now and it's a good time to take a break or relax.

Origin:

Although the exact time and manner of its origin remain uncertain, it is believed that the idiom "Let's call it a day" has a history that extends back to the early years of the 20th century.

Example:

We've explored the park and had lots of fun. Let's call it a day and come back tomorrow.

Every rose has its thorn

Meaning:

Sometimes even beautiful things have something unpleasant or difficult about them.

Origin:

In the 1800s in England and America, people grew pretty red flowers. The flowers had pointy bits that could hurt hands when picking them.

Example:

Life is like a garden where every rose has its thorn, teaching us to embrace both the good and the difficult.

Silence is golden

Meaning:

Sometimes, staying quiet can be really valuable and important.

Origin:

The origin of the expression dates back to the 16th century. Among gold miners, words implying the importance and value of silence began to be used.

Example:

In a library, silence is like a superpower that helps you become the golden bookworm.

Clothes make the man

Meaning:

The way you dress can show others what kind of person you are. It means that your clothes can tell a story about you without using words.

Origin:

The origin of this expression dates back to the 14th century. In medieval England, social status and wealth became prominently displayed through clothing.

Example:

The scientist's lab coat and goggles showed that he was a smart and capable person, just like clothes make the man.

No man is an island

Meaning:

We are all interconnected and rely on each other in various ways. No individual can thrive or exist in isolation.

Origin:

The origin of this expression dates back to the 17th century and is attributed to the English poet and clergyman John Donne. It gained popularity after Donne used this phrase in a quotation found in his work, "Meditation XVII."

Example:

We can learn from each other because no man is an island.

A watched pot never boils

Meaning:

Sometimes, when we wait and watch for something to happen, it feels like it takes a very long time.

Origin:

According to a theory, in English cuisine, the feeling of time passing slowly while waiting by the pot when cooking dishes that require boiling water might have led to the expression "A watched pot never boils."

Example:

Checking my email every few minutes for a response, it seemed a watched pot never boils.

Hit the hay

Meaning:

Time to go to bed and get some rest.

Origin:

The origin of this expression is uncertain but it may date back to the 19th century.

According to a theory, the term "hay" refers to beds filled with straw in the olden days. Sleeping on a straw-filled bed meant going to sleep.

Example:

After a long day of playing, it's time to hit the hay and rest.

Don't count your chickens

Meaning:

Be patient and wait for things to happen before celebrating or being sure about them.

Origin:

In the 1500s in England, farming chickens was common. Farmers would count eggs to estimate profits from chicks hatching. But not all eggs yielded healthy chicks.

Example:

My brother was sure he would win but I told him don't count your chickens.

Needle in a haystack

Meaning:

Finding something very difficult or nearly impossible because it's hidden or lost among many other things.

Origin:

In the 1500s in England, people made needles by hand. They packaged needles in big piles of hay. It was very difficult to find a single needle in the hay. It took a long time.

Example:

Finding a tiny puzzle piece among a pile of other puzzle pieces is like finding a needle in a haystack.

Better safe than sorry

Meaning:

Avoiding risky things is better. Taking precautions and being careful is smarter than feeling regretful.

Origin:

In the 1700s in England, there were many accidents and injuries. People started to be more careful. They said "It is better to be safe than take a risk." Over time, this saying became very common.

Example:

Taking an umbrella with you on a cloudy day is better safe than sorry.

Off the hook

Meaning:

When a problem or task is resolved, it means it has been taken care of or solved. It's like when a tricky situation is no longer a concern, and you can feel relieved and relaxed.

Origin:

In the late 1800s in America, fishermen would hook big fish onto their boats. If a fish got free of the hook, it was off the hook.

Example:

Emily was worried about being late, but the bus came early, and she was off the hook.

Take a rain check

Meaning:

When someone invites you to do something, but you can't go, you can ask to do it another time. It's like keeping the plan on hold. It means you're interested, but not right now.

Origin:

In the 1920s in America, sporting events would be delayed if it rained. Fans could not get a refund for missing the game. Instead they were given a "rain check" ticket to use for the next game.

Example:

Mom asked if I wanted to bake cookies, but I had to take a rain check because we ran out of ingredients.

All eyes on me

Meaning:

Everyone is watching you and paying attention to only you. You are the center of focus now.

Origin:

In the 1890s in America, circuses and vaudeville shows were popular entertainment. Performers would try to stand out and get the audience's attention. One successful performer would say things like "Everyone is looking at me" to draw the crowd in.

Example:

I painted a colorful picture, and everyone's eyes were on my artwork.

All that jazz

Meaning:

It means everything related to something or everything that goes with a specific thing.

Origin:

In the 1920s in America, jazz music was becoming popular. People would listen to jazz bands play complex songs at clubs and concerts. The music had lots of different instruments and sounds. Fans enjoyed the excitement of it all.

Example:

We went to the zoo and saw lions, giraffes, monkeys, and all that jazz.

Fortune favors the bold

Meaning:

Taking risks and being brave increases your chances of success.

Origin:

In ancient Greece 500 BC, a philosopher named Terentius first said this phrase. At that time, brave heroes were often successful. Over the years it came to mean that courageous people will be lucky.

Example:

My sister raised her hand to answer a difficult question in class, and fortune favored the bold because she got it right.

Haste makes waste

Meaning:

When you do things too quickly, you can end up making mistakes or wasting what you have.

Origin:

In the late 1500s in England, people wasted resources when rushing jobs. Working slowly and carefully meant less waste. Over time it came to mean that going too fast causes mistakes.

Example:

We cleaned our room fast but mom said haste makes waste.

Out of sight, out of mind

Meaning:

When you can't see something, you tend to forget about it or stop thinking about it.

Origin:

In the 1800s in the United States, people tended to focus only on what was right in front of them each day. If something was not in their sight, it was easier to forget about later on.

Example:

If you put your toys in a box and close it, you forget about playing with them. Out of sight, out of mind!

You reap what you sow

Meaning:

What you do has what comes back to you. Good stuff you do means good stuff for you. Bad stuff you do means bad stuff for you later.

Origin:

The saying comes from the Bible in the 1st century AD. It said your actions will have results, like farmers get wheat from wheat seeds, not other grains

Example:

When you practice playing the piano every day, you will become a skilled pianist. It's true, you reap what you sow.

Put your best foot forward

Meaning:

Do your very best and show your skills when you try something new or important.

Origin:

In the 1500s in England, people wanted to make a good first step. They thought starting with your strong foot looked best.

Example:

If you're helping in the kitchen, follow the recipe carefully and make something delicious. Put your best foot forward!

Walk on eggshells

Meaning:

Be extra careful and cautious in your words and actions so as not to upset or bother someone.

Origin:

In North America in the early 1900s, farmers walked around eggs so they wouldn't crack. They had to move gently.

Example:

When you're handling a delicate flower, hold it gently and avoid crushing its petals. You have to walk on eggshells.

Easier said than done

Meaning:

Talk is easy, doing is hard. Thinking takes less work than acting. Words come easy, real life is tough.

Origin:

In the 1700s, settlers in America faced hard times. Talking about things didn't capture reality. Suggestions didn't get the true problems.

Example:

Talking about being patient is simple, but actually waiting calmly can be difficult. It's easier said than done.

Apples and oranges

Meaning:

Some things are too different to match or compare. You can't talk about one like the other. Things need to be alike for a good look side by side.

Origin:

In the 1800s in Europe and North America, apples and oranges seemed very different. Apples grew there but oranges came from other places. Comparing them made little sense as they were so unlike.

Example:

Riding a bike and driving a car are different ways to travel. They're like apples and oranges.

Buy a pig in a poke

Meaning:

The idiom means to buy something without knowing its true value or quality.

Origin:

In 1400s England, some sellers tried to trick with bags. Pigs were sold unseen in pokes to hide faults. So people didn't know if sick or fine. This became a sign for secret problems in deals.

Example:

Lisa traded her favorite trading card for a mystery pack, but she was disappointed with what she got. She realized she had "bought a pig in a poke."

Any port in a storm

Meaning:

When things get really hard or there's a problem, sometimes we have to use whatever option is available, even if it's not perfect.

Origin:

In 1600s sea voyages in Europe and North America, ships in bad weather entered any close harbor for shelter even if not the best. "Any port" meant saving crew over destination.

Example:

When the power goes out, any flashlight will help you see in the dark. It's like any light in a storm.

Turn over a new leaf

Meaning:

To start fresh and make positive changes in your actions or behavior. It's like turning the page of a book to begin a new chapter where you make better choices and improve yourself.

Origin:

In 1500s Western Europe, the new year and falling foliage were signs of change. Leaving the past and starting fresh meant cleaning the calendar slate.

Example:

Jake realized he needed to turn over a new leaf and eat healthier foods instead of junk food.

As good as gold

Meaning:

Always kind, well-behaved, and trustworthy, like a shining star.

Origin:

Phase begun Western Europe 1800s when gold meant top value. Calling kid "gold" described perfectly behaved, matching gold's status then.

Example:

Max always shares his toys with his friends and helps them when they're in need. He's as good as gold.

Add fuel to the fire

Meaning:

Make a bad situation even more heated or intense, like making a disagreement or fight escalate.

Origin:

Phrase from 1700s Europe. Literally meant adding wood/coal to make flames stronger. It grew as a saying to mean worsening issues, like fuel boosts fires.

Example:

During lunchtime, Sam accidentally spilled juice on Jake's new shirt, which added fuel to the fire of their ongoing rivalry.

Show your true colors

Meaning:

To reveal your real character or personality, like showing who you really are on the inside.

Origin:

Phrase from 1500s Europe sail era. Flags identified ship country/side far at sea then. Crucial to distinguish allies/others in fights by flags.

Example:

She used to be impatient with her classmates, but when she started offering help and guidance, she showed her true colors.

Go bananas

Meaning:

It means to feel incredibly happy and excited. It's like when something wonderful or surprising happens and you can't help but smile and feel full of energy.

Origin:

Phrase from North America 1930s referring to chimpanzees/monkeys behaving very energetically when overly excited. Americans used it for people acting completely unpredictably.

Example:

When the music started, the kids went bananas and started dancing like crazy.

At sixes and sevens

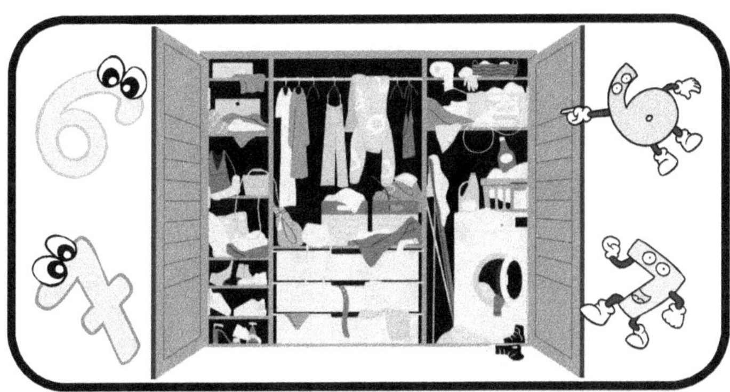

Meaning:

When everything is in a state of chaos and confusion, it's like a big mess where nothing is in the right order.

Origin:

12th-century England had guilds for craftsmen and merchants. One guild, "sixes," worked with weaving, while another, "sevens," focused on leatherwork. Disputes and rivalries between these guilds led to the expression "at sixes and sevens," meaning disorder and disagreement.

Example:

The puzzle pieces were all at sixes and sevens, making it hard to complete.

Wishful thinking

Meaning:

Hoping for something to happen or be true, even though it may be unlikely or unrealistic.

Origin:

Phrase from 1800s Europe referring to making good outlooks from wants more than proofs. Rather than plans grounded in facts, it meant hoping problems solve by dreams alone.

Example:

Alex wished to become a professional basketball player without practicing, but he knew it was just wishful thinking.

Pull someone's leg

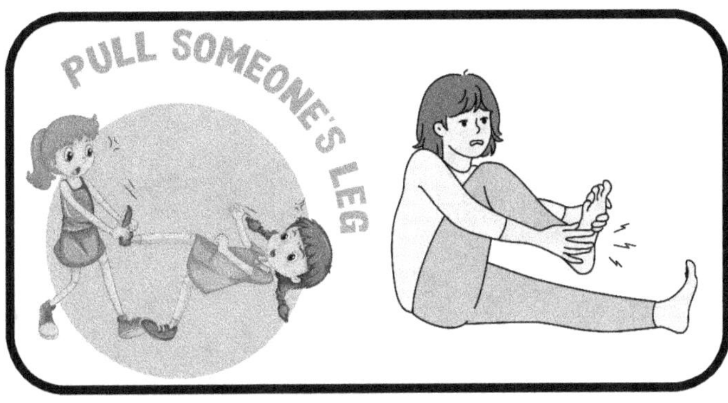

Meaning:

Teasing or joking with someone playfully, making them believe something that is not true.

Origin:

Phrase from 1800s Britain, North America referring to literally yanking a leg usually as joke. Leg pulling meant startling or tricking for fun. Over time it grew as metaphor to describe teasing or playing jokes on people.

Example:

Mom said she saw a purple elephant in the living room, pulling our legs and making us laugh.

Clean your plate

Meaning:

It means to finish all the food on your plate without leaving any remaining food.

Origin:

Phrase from late 1800s Western Europe, North America. Then, food wastage discouraged due to farm/homestead limitations in those areas. Children taught there to eat all served showing gratitude and avoiding leftover food loss.

Example:

The babysitter encouraged the kids to clean their plates and praised them for finishing their meals.

Keep your nose clean

Meaning:

To maintain good behavior, stay away from trouble, and avoid engaging in wrong or harmful actions.

Origin:

Phrase from early 1900s Britain, North America referring to literally keeping nose/face clean from dirt as sign of cleanliness. A cleaned nose implied hygiene and decency. Later it grew metaphorical to mean avoiding issues or bad acts.

Example:

Like a detective, sniff out trouble and keep your nose clean from any mischief.

Beat the clock

Meaning:

Try to complete a task or activity before a set time limit expires. The goal is to finish quickly and efficiently, racing against the passing time.

Origin:

Phrase emerged early 1900s North America referring to racing versus finishing ahead of timed clock at county events.

Example:

Can you beat the clock and finish your snack before the TV show starts?

Bread and butter

Meaning:

This expression refers to someone's main or primary source of income or livelihood. It represents the key work or activity through which someone consistently earns money.

Origin:

Phrase originated 1700s Western Europe notably Britain referring to bread and butter like cheese being basic foods for average class survival then.

Example:

Selling lemonade at the fair is Johnny's bread and butter for making money.

Learn the ropes

Meaning:

To acquire skills and knowledge for a new job or situation.

Origin:

Phrase from 1800s Britain referring to sailors obtaining skills from controlling sails, anchors managing ropes on ships. Novices grasped expertise in ropes' hands-on use. Later it metaphorically meant learning procedures for any new role.

Example:

Emma joined a theater group to learn the ropes of acting and performing on stage.

White elephant

Meaning:

The phrase refers to something that is costly or difficult to handle but doesn't have much practical value.

Origin:

In 1500s Southeast Asia, royal families gifted rare elephants. Elephants expensive to care for but not useful. This caused financial problems for receivers. Over time, the phrase meant things costly to maintain though having no value.

Example:

Alice's huge toy collection became a white elephant because she never played with most of them.

Lucky break

Meaning:

A "lucky break" is when something unexpectedly good happens to someone that helps them reach their goals or achieve success.

Origin:

The term emerged in late 1800s North America referring to fortunate random events like unexpected outcomes in games seen as beneficial.

Example:

Sarah wanted a piece of cake, and she got a lucky break when there was an extra slice left.

Count sheep

Meaning:

When you're having trouble falling asleep, you can imagine something calming and repetitive in your head.

Origin:

The phrase emerged in early 1900s Europe from shepherds counting their flock at night. This was to ensure none went missing and all were accounted for before rest. The repetitive nature of counting was believed to induce sleepiness.

Example:

Emily had trouble falling asleep, so she decided to count sheep in her mind.

Mind reader

Meaning:

When someone knows your thoughts and feelings without you telling them, it's like they have a special power to understand you.

Origin:

Origin of "mind reader" is linked to ancient stories about people who could understand thoughts. Its exact source remains unknown.

Example:

When Tim is sad, his mom seems to be a mind reader and knows how to cheer him up.

Hold water

Meaning:

When something makes sense and doesn't have any problems or mistakes, it's like a strong bucket that doesn't have any leaks. It's reliable and trustworthy.

Origin:

The term emerged 1700s among seafarers meaning watertight vessels. By 1800s meant logical arguments withstand scrutiny.

Example:

Jane's explanation for why she got an A on her test held water because she studied hard and knew the material well.

Hat in hand

Meaning:

It means they are being very polite and showing that they appreciate the other person.

Origin:

The term originated in late medieval Europe where removing one's hat signified respect, especially to superiors. Literally holding one's hat humbly indicated submission notably when requesting favors.

Example:

Emily approached the principal with hat in hand to ask for permission to organize a school event.

Tip of the iceberg

Meaning:

Sometimes, what we can see or know about something is only a small part of the whole picture. It's like seeing the very top of an iceberg sticking out of the water.

Origin:

The term emerged in early 1900s northern Europe and North America to describe Arctic shipping risks. Sailors there knew most of an iceberg lay underwater, with only its small "tip" visible.

Example:

The small dot on the map is just the tip of the iceberg. There's a whole city to explore beyond that.

Use your loaf

Meaning:

It means to think carefully or use your brain to solve a problem or make a good decision. It's like using your thinking power to figure things out.

Origin:

The idiom emerged in early 1900s Britain, literally referring to utilizing one's brain or common sense like using bread (loaf) to sustain oneself.

Example:

The math problem was a piece of cake for him; he solved it in seconds.

Eat like a bird

Meaning:

It means to eat very little or have a small appetite, like a bird. It's like eating small amounts of food or being satisfied with small portions.

Origin:

The idiom emerged early 1800s from bird feeding behaviors observed in regions like US/UK, with species eating small frequent meals while selectively foraging.

Example:

My little brother eats like a bird, he never finishes his plate.

It's not rocket science

Meaning:

When something is not difficult or complicated, we say that it's easy to understand or do. It's like saying that it doesn't require advanced knowledge or skills.

Origin:

This idiom emerged in the US during the 1960s Space Race, referring to the immensely complex engineering of rockets/spacecraft. Rocket science was viewed as remarkably difficult, advanced work.

Example:

Following a recipe to bake cookies is simple; it's not rocket science to make delicious treats.

Ship has sailed

Meaning:

It means that an opportunity or chance has passed and it's too late to take advantage of it.

Origin:

Emerging in the 18th-19th century maritime trading era in nations like the UK, US and others, this term originally referred to literally missing travel opportunities by ships departing ports/docks in places like British and American cities.

Example:

Emily wanted to see her favorite band perform, but all the tickets were sold out. The ship had sailed.

Know your onions

Meaning:

When someone knows a lot about a particular subject or skill, we say they 'know their onions.

Origin:

The exact origins are uncertain but likely stem from historical onion farming and trade, a major industry especially in countries like the UK and Europe. In the 19th century UK, the term "onion" began referring to expert farmers knowledgeable about varietals and practices.

Example:

Jack can name all the planets in our solar system. He knows his onions about space.

Small potatoes

Meaning:

When we say something is 'small potatoes,' it means it is not very important or significant. It's like saying it's not a big deal or not worth much attention.

Origin:

Emerging late 19th century in US-Canada, this idiom derived from potatoes' importance then as crops-food, and potato size reflecting farmers' statuses, with "small potatoes" literally an undesirable small harvest.

Example:

Getting a small stain on your shirt is small potatoes because you can wash it and wear it again.

Lemons into lemonade

Meaning:

When something bad happens, making lemons into lemonade means finding a way to turn it into something good or positive.

Origin:

This idiom originated in early 19th century United States referring to the actual practice of making refreshing lemonade from surplus lemons, an abundant citrus at the time.

Example:

When it rained on our picnic day, we played fun indoor games instead. We turned lemons into lemonade!

Eagle eye

Meaning:

This idiom means to have the ability to see things clearly and in detail, just like an eagle's sharp vision.

Origin:

This idiom originated from the phrase "having an eagle's eye" used in ancient Greek and Roman culture, where eagles were believed to have exceptionally keen vision able to discern small prey from long distances.

Example:

Sarah's eagle eye spotted the tiny bird in the tree.

Look before you leap

Meaning:

This sentence emphasizes the importance of considering the possible consequences before engaging in any action.

Origin:

This idiom is traced to Aesop's Fables written 620-564 BC, specifically the tale of a mouse sighting bread and cheese in a trap yet failing to consider danger prior to impulsively leaping towards the food.

Example:

The hiker paused to look before leaping over the rocky path.

Drag feet

Meaning:

This idiom suggests being slow or hesitant in completing a task, indicating reluctance or unwillingness to act promptly.

Origin:

This idiom dates back to early 19th century Britain, originating from the actual practice of shackling prisoners' or criminals' feet with heavy chains and weights during transport.

Example:

He always drags his feet when it's time to clean his room.

Time will tell

Meaning:

This sentence conveys the idea that the complete truth or result of a situation will become apparent over time.

Origin:

This idiom emerged 1600s in English cultures believing time would resolve uncertainty. Derived from time's revelation of hidden facts, patience was counseled over rush to decide ambiguous topics within linguistic communities.

Example:

We don't know if the new restaurant is good, but time will tell.